Harrogate

MARK REID

Dalesman Publishing Company Ltd
Stable Courtyard, Broughton Hall,
Skipton, North Yorkshire BD23 3AZ
www.dalesman.co.uk

First Edition 2000

Text © Mark Reid
Illustrations © John Ives

Maps by Jeremy Ashcroft and Harry Salisbury

Cover: Harrogate town centre and war memorial by Mike Kipling

A British Library Cataloguing in Publication record
is available for this book

ISBN 1 85568 172 2

Printed by Amadeus Press, Huddersfield

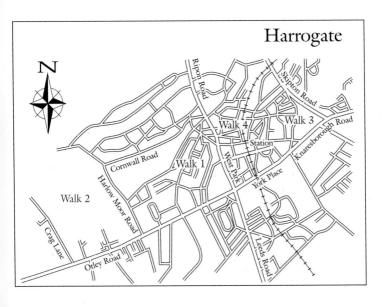

Introduction

Despite growing up in Harrogate, attending the Grammar School, playing football on The Stray, going to functions at the Lounge Hall or one of the many hotels, and even tasting the sulphur water on a school trip, I must confess that I took little notice of my surroundings – I just got on with my life. The time spent researching this book has brought new life to familiar places; it is as though I have moved to a different town. It is amazing just how little you know a place until you actually start to look a bit closer – I never knew that Harrogate was England's most historic Spa Town with a globally unique variety of mineral waters – shame on me! At every corner is a wealth of history and beautiful architecture with the magnificent open land of The Stray at its heart. When I walk through the town I look at The Stray in a different way for this was once the common land of a vast Royal hunting forest – fuel for the imagination indeed. In fact I look at everything in Harrogate in a different way now, the immense Victorian villas, incredibly luxurious hotels, elegant streets, shops and gardens. Armed with a little knowledge, our world is a wonderful place to explore and discover – the world immediately around you.

History

John A. Ivo S / '00.

Harrogate is arguably the finest town in Yorkshire. Sitting proudly on a breezy shelf of land at the very heart of the British Isles, it is a refined town of elegant buildings, imposing hotels, antique shops, open parkland and flower beds; it is the original 'Spa Town'. And what a wonderful place it is to live, with the thriving cosmopolitan city of Leeds, the historic cities of York and Ripon and the magnificent Yorkshire Dales only a short distance away.

The town is made up of the ancient villages of High and Low Harrogate, both of which still retain their own separate identities. High Harrogate sits on top of the plateau and grew from the original medieval settlement of Harrogate that existed along the edges of the old common of the Royal Forest of Knaresborough, part of which now forms The Stray. Low Harrogate is clustered around several small valleys to the north of this plateau centred on the Royal Pump Room that stands over the Old Sulphur Well. Nowhere else in the world has such a diverse range of mineral springs in such close proximity. Within a two-mile radius there are eighty-eight springs of varying degrees of mineral content from strong sulphur to pure chalybeate (iron), thirty-six of which rise in the Bogs Field area of the Valley Gardens.

The springs rise from the underlying magma of igneous rock deep beneath the Earth's crust passing through various layers of minerals along the way before surfacing through faults in the carboniferous rock strata exposed by volcanic activity. These waters, which are over 20,000 years old, are Magmatic or Plutonic and have never existed as rain. For almost 400 years Harrogate was the foremost spa town in England, if not the world; however, since the Royal Baths closed for Spa treatment in 1969, the town has reinvented itself as a busy conference and exhibition centre. Many of the historic spa buildings, amenities and luxurious hotels remain as well as the superb flower gardens and, of course, the wonderful Stray.

The name of Harrogate is somewhat of a mystery as it is either derived from 'Herehlaw-gate' meaning 'the road to Harlow or Soldier's Hill' or from 'Haywra-gate' meaning 'the road to Haverah Park', once a Royal hunting preserve within the vast Forest of Knaresborough. First mentioned in 1332, the settlement of Harrogate remained a small, dispersed farming community within this Forest lying just to the north of the extensive common lands. All this changed in 1571 when William Slingsby 'discovered' a chalybeate spring on this common land at what is now Tewit Well. A well travelled man, he recognised the similarity of the water to that of the famous Spa in Belgium and had the area paved and walled so that the waters could be utilised for medicinal purposes and brought it to the attention of Dr Bright, physician to Queen Elizabeth I.

Tewit Well was the first 'spa' in the British Isles. The medicinal qualities of this spring became widely known following the publication of Dr. Edmund Deane's *Spadacrene Anglica* or 'The English Spa' in 1626: "It cheereth and reviveth the spirits, strengtheneth the stomacke, causeth a good and quicke appetite, and furthereth digestion." Exaggerated to almost 'cure all' status, doctors soon began prescribing the waters for their patients. Other springs were discovered, including St John's Well in 1631, which was close to the village of High Harrogate. However, facilities and amenities for drinkers were few and many people stayed at the neighbouring town of Knaresborough.

By the mid-17th century the 'Spa Season' began to develop with several boarding houses and inns built in High Harrogate on the border of the old common along Granby Road and Devonshire Place. The earliest of these was the Queens Hotel (now the Cedar Court Hotel) which dates from circa 1687, as well as the Granby and Dragon which also both date from the late 17th century. As the popularity of Harrogate's waters grew, so did the number of books by doctors extolling their virtues. One of the most important of these was by a Leeds doctor called George Neale who wrote *Spadacrene Eboracensis* which appeared in Dr. Short's *History of the Mineral Waters* in 1734 and advocated bathing in heated sulphur water. The sulphur springs of Low Harrogate were now gaining in popularity due to a shift in fashion for sulphur water as well as an increasing belief in their curative powers for rheumatism, gout and digestive problems.

The oldest hotel in Low Harrogate is the Crown Inn, established in 1740 by Joseph Thackwray and situated adjacent to the Old Sulphur Well. Soon lodging houses, inns and hotels began to radiate from this central point along Cold Bath Road, Well Hill, Swan Road and West Park.

Harrogate became a fashionable place to spend the Season especially due to its burgeoning social life, which in itself became an attraction. The demand for new facilities to entertain these well-heeled visitors increased and so a church was built on The Stray in 1749, a dome constructed over St John's Well in 1786, a

7

theatre opened in Church Square in 1788 and a racecourse laid out on The Stray in 1793 – all of these developments were in High Harrogate. When it was proposed to divide up and sell off the Royal Forest of Knaresborough in the 1760s, there was great public concern about the future of the wells, which lay on open common land. However, following the Enclosure Act of 1770, steps were taken to protect the open walks between the wells and an Award of 1778 set aside two hundred acres of common land to provide free public access to the springs. The Stray has been jealously guarded by the people of Harrogate ever since and is protected by Act of Parliament.

The discovery of new chalybeate springs in Low Harrogate meant that by the beginning of the 19th century the focus began to switch to this part of Harrogate. Improved turnpike roads, prosperity and the fashion for Spa treatment meant a surge in the number of visitors during the Season in the early 1800s. Visitors ranged from the sick and diseased to people who came as part of the social circuit – everybody from royalty to the very poor. Lack of local government meant that any improvement to the wells or the provision of public amenities rested on the shoulders of private individuals. Hotels and lodgings collected donations to help the poor take advantage of the baths, out of which the idea for the Royal Bath Hospital grew, which opened in 1826. In 1804 public subscription meant that improvements could be made to the Old Sulphur Well, with a new stone canopy constructed over it in 1807, and the Promenade Rooms opened in 1806. Several imposing Georgian and Regency hotels and lodging houses were also built at this time, many of which still stand, although Low Harrogate was essentially a rural settlement comprised predominantly of inns and hotels such as the Swan, George, Crescent, Crown, White Hart, Wellington, Binns' and the houses of Well Hill and Prospect Row.

There was a similar picture in High Harrogate with hotels such as the Hope Inn, Bay Horse, Granby, Queen and Dragon as well as a handful of houses fronting The Stray. Local businessman John Williams was the first to recognise the need for large-scale spa amenities and so had The Victoria Baths constructed in 1832 behind the old Crescent Inn in what is now Crescent Gardens, a luxurious suite of baths housed in a building of Greek Ionic design that set the tone for the development of Harrogate. Others were quick to follow. Joseph Thackwray, the owner of the Crown Hotel, built a magnificent suite of baths in 1834 adjacent to his hotel. His Montpellier Baths provided visitors with music, gardens and tile and marble baths.

The finest Spa building in Harrogate was built in 1835 for John Williams over the newly discovered Cheltenham Spring. His Royal Promenade and Cheltenham Pumproom, later the Royal Spa Concert Rooms, was a masterpiece of classical architecture with six acres of gardens and a boating lake fed by a stream that also carried the town's sewage! However, a simple act of greed was to completely change the way the town operated. In 1835 Thackwray began searching for new sulphur springs and in doing so sank a well close to the public springs of the Old Sulphur Well affecting the flow of water, contrary to the Enclosure Act of 1770. This caused outrage and legal action was brought against Thackwray who was ordered to provide this new spring free to the public. More importantly, this highlighted the growing gap between private and public supply and led to the formation of the Harrogate Improvement Commissioners in 1841 with the main aim of improving the public wells. This they did with the opening of the Royal Pump Room over the Old Sulphur Well in 1842; the old domed canopy was moved to cover the Tewit Well.

The arrival of the railway in 1848 heralded the real boom years of Harrogate when a branch line from Church Fenton brought visitors to the old Brunswick Station. Competition was fierce during this period of Railway Mania and a rival line was completed between Thirsk and Leeds in 1849 via Starbeck with a branch line to Knaresborough and York. Harrogate's central station was opened in 1862 following the construction of a connecting line between the Thirsk to Leeds line and the Church Fenton branch line.

Harrogate was still very much a rural village of two parts with little paving, no sewage treatment and no direct road between the two villages, but development was about to happen. The arrival of the railway meant that Harrogate grew from a seasonal spa town into a fashionable commuter town for the emerging wealthy businessmen of the industrial West Riding of Yorkshire. New large housing developments were built between the old villages of High and Low Harrogate, in particular Victoria Park, West End Park and from the 1880s the Franklin Estate, Alexandra Park, Dragon Estate and the Duchy Estate, much of which stands today as some of the finest examples of planned Victorian urban development in the world.

From the 1860s the Improvement Commissioners gradually began to take a more active role in the government of Harrogate with the provision of street paving, sewage treatment, road building and the construction of public spa buildings, although gas and water supply remained in private ownership for many more years. They bought the old Victoria Baths and Crescent Inn in 1870 and built the New Victoria Baths on the site in 1871. The Market Hall was opened in 1874 and Bower Road and North Park Road connecting High and Low Harrogate were built in 1875, although such direct roads between the two old settlements should have been their first priority.

Harrogate became a municipal borough in 1884 after which things began to change at an incredible pace. The Council took over the management of The Stray in 1893 from the Straygate Owners who had grazing rights, the Valley Gardens were laid out between the Royal Pump Room and Bogs Field in 1887 and they took over the water supply and established the municipal electricity works in 1897. As the number of Spa therapies grew, the Council decided to build a new suite of baths on the site of the newly acquired Montpellier Baths and in 1897 the Royal Baths were opened, the most advanced centre for hydrotherapy in the world offering a score of different treatments. The Council realised that social amenities were just as important as medicinal ones and so acquired the Royal Spa Concert Rooms in 1896 to provide quality entertainment for visitors. Such was its success that plans were drawn up for a larger concert hall adjacent to the Spa Rooms and in 1902 the Kursaal, later renamed the Royal Hall, opened its doors.

The private sector invested heavily in the town with the construction of luxurious hotels on an immense scale such as the Majestic (1900) and Grand (1903) as well as the elegant Grand Opera House. Private and public development continued up until the outbreak of war in 1914. This was Harrogate's heyday with King Manuel of Portugal, Queen Alexandra, Prince Henry of Prussia and Prince Christopher of Greece as well as countless other aristocrats all visiting in 1911 and over 75,000 visitors a year coming to take the waters, avail themselves of the many treatments on offer and to soak up the social life.

Life was never the same after the Great War, although the years following 1918 saw a surge in visitors as people sought to forget the terrors of the war. The Spa routine continued as it had always done with the roads surrounding the Royal Pump Room closed during the morning to allow people to promenade along the streets and listen to the band in Crescent Gardens. The entertainment flourished at the Spa Rooms, Royal Hall and Winter Gardens; however, the financial crisis of the late 1920s had a great effect on Harrogate. The Victoria Baths closed in 1930 after which they were remodelled into the present day Council Offices and entertainment was cut at the Royal Hall and Spa Rooms. The Council embarked on ambitious schemes to revitalise the fortunes of the town with the building of the Sun Pavilion and Sun Colonnade in 1933 along with the remodelling of the Valley Gardens and extensions to the Royal Baths in 1936. But this inter-war period also saw medical opinion turn away from Spa treatment and the new generation began to turn their backs on the Victorian lifestyle associated with Harrogate.

The Council decided that the way forward was diversification and so began to promote the town as a conference centre during the late 1930s, which led to the greatest act of vandalism in the history of Harrogate with the demolition of the Royal Spa Concert Rooms in 1939. Many of Harrogate's hotels were requisitioned by the Government during the Second World War, some of which remained in their ownership until recently. The emergence of the National Health Service in 1948 heralded the terminal decline of Spa treatment. The Royal Pump Room closed after the war becoming a restaurant for a while and then a museum in 1953 and the final nail in the coffin of the Harrogate Spa came in 1969 with the closure of the Royal Baths, although its Turkish Baths are still open.

Harrogate is now a very successful exhibition and conference centre with several major events such as the Toy Fair, Bridal Wear Fair and Liberal Democrats' Conference ensuring that the hotels are full. Harrogate also hosts several other regular events such as the Spring Flower Show, Great Yorkshire Show and Harrogate International Festival. Extensive exhibition halls were built on the site of the Spa Rooms in 1959 and the conspicuous and controversial brick-built International Centre rose over Low Harrogate in the early 1980s. Harrogate is beginning to wake up to the importance of its unique heritage with more and more sympathetic new architecture and a growing interest in the old Spa of Harrogate with plans to redevelop many of its historic Spa buildings as well as to revitalise the fortunes of the once famous Harrogate Mineral Water.

Low Harrogate

John A. I.S., '00.

(1) *From the back of the Royal Pump Room Museum walk along Crown Place, across Crescent Road then head along Swan Road to reach the Old Swan Hotel.*

The elegant copper-domed **Royal Pump Room** stands proudly above the Old Sulphur Well, the strongest sulphur spring in the world, and also known as 'The Stinking Well'. Designed by Isaac Shutt of the Swan Hotel, this building dates from 1842 and was the first project of the newly-created Harrogate Improvement

13

Commissioners and replaced the earlier domed canopy which was moved to cover the Tewit Well. The elaborate glass and iron annexe was built in 1913 and opened by the Lord Mayor of London to relieve overcrowding during the morning rush to take the waters; in 1926 over 1500 glasses were served in one morning!

The decline of spa treatment meant that the Royal Pump Room was no longer used for its intended purpose after the Second World War and the building now houses a fascinating museum. The old well-heads can still be seen in the basement at what was once the original ground level, protected by glass screens due to the overpowering sulphur fumes. At first glance the surface of the spring looks like concrete, but this is due to the high mineral content of the water – look out for the occasional bubble!

These waters were served from communal ladles by women, the most famous of whom was Betty Lupton, The Queen of the Wells, who dispensed the waters for many years until her death in 1843 at the age of 83. A free tap outside ensures that there is always a supply; however, I recommend a visit to the museum followed by a small glass of sulphur water – the trick is not to smell the water before drinking it, just swallow it in one go – it is hard to imagine that people once drank up to two pints a day for three weeks! There are plans to develop a bottling plant at Harlow Hill for Harrogate Mineral Water, which will ensure the tradition of Harrogate's famous waters will continue.

The Royal Pump Room backs on to **Crown Place**, which boasts some fine Victorian buildings built during the 1880s by George Dawson, one of Harrogate's most influential men. This was where in 1835 Joseph Thackwray, owner of The Crown, sank a well in search of new sulphur springs, contrary to the Enclosure Act of 1770, and in doing so affected the flow to the public sulphur wells. Legal action was brought against Thackwray by many of the town's hoteliers following which he was ordered to provide this new spring free to the public. This incident highlighted the importance of the public mineral waters as well as the growing gap between private and public spa amenities and

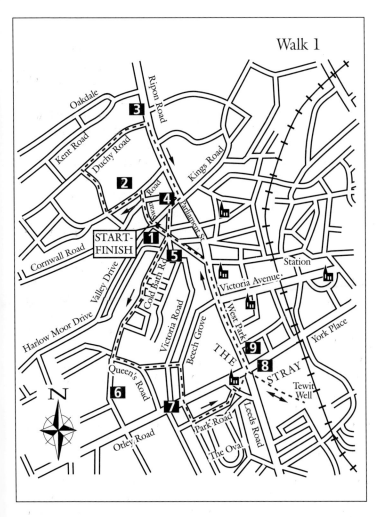

Walk 1

was the catalyst in the formation of the Harrogate Improvement Commissioners in 1841.

Hales Bar is a superb example of an early Victorian public house and retains many original features including gas lighting, brass bar-mounted cigar lighters and cases of stuffed birds. The fact that

Hales Bar

this pub has a cellar means that it pre-dates the Enclosure Act of 1770, almost certainly from the mid 17th century when a handful of inns were established adjacent to the Old Sulphur Well. Originally known as The Promenade Inn, it changed names to Hodgson's and then Hales Bar during the 1880s.

Several superb Georgian lodging houses still stand on **Well Hill**, once favoured by wealthy visitors who preferred these more attentive establishments to the larger hotels. The small grassed area in front of these houses is actually a detached portion of The Stray. **The Mercer Art Gallery** is housed in the old Promenade Rooms, built by public subscription in 1806 to provide visitors to the Old Sulphur Well with somewhere to relax and generally socialise after taking the waters. The building was modified during the 1870s and served for a time as the Town Hall and as a theatre where some famous names performed including Oscar Wilde and Lillie Langtry. This was also where the Improvement Commissioners met for the first time in 1841. The building became an art gallery in 1991 providing a permanent exhibition for Harrogate's fine collection of art and antiquities, and admission is free.

The Old Swan Hotel began life as a small inn during the early 18th century when it was known as the Swan and has subsequently grown over the centuries into one of Harrogate's finest hotels, being extensively rebuilt in 1820 and 1878 when it became known as the Harrogate Hydropathic. When Agatha Christie famously 'disappeared' for eleven days during 1926 as she tried to escape from personal problems, she was discovered by reporters at the Harrogate Hydropathic, the story of which was later made into the film *Agatha* starring Dustin Hoffman and Vanessa Redgrave. As with many of Harrogate's hotels, the Hydropathic was requisitioned during the Second World War reopening again as the Old Swan Hotel in 1948. During my student days I worked here as a porter which meant that, apart from carrying suitcases, I had to perform the job of Hornblower. Dressed in a cloak and top hat I announced the arrival of coaches of the motorised variety, laden with American tourists, with a blow of a long, brass posting horn, a tradition that dates back to the old coaching days.

(2) *From the Old Swan turn left along York Road then take the second turning on the right along Clarence Drive to reach Duchy Road. Turn right along Duchy Road and follow it all the way to reach the busy Ripon Road.*

The Duchy Estate covers 54 acres of land to the north-west of Harrogate – a late Victorian development of imposing houses and villas set in spacious grounds, many of which have servants quarters and coach houses. Prior to the Enclosure Act of 1770 the Forest of Knaresborough belonged to the Crown through the Duchy of Lancaster; however, when the Forest was enclosed the Crown retained a great deal of land to the west of Harrogate which later provided valuable building land for the wealthy middle classes of the West Riding. The bracing air, spa waters and healthy lifestyle of Harrogate has attracted many private schools to the area including the renowned **Harrogate Ladies College**, whose Chapel was built using stones from the old St Mary's Church of Low Harrogate following its demolition after 1904. Near to the junction of Duchy Road and Clarence Drive stands Harrogate's most beautiful church dedicated to **St Wilfrid**. Designed by the famous Temple Moore in Early English style and constructed using soft honey-coloured stone, this fine church was consecrated in 1908.

(3) *Turn right down Ripon Road into the town centre to reach Crescent Gardens opposite the Royal Hall.*

The **Cairn Hotel** was originally known as the Cairn Hydro when it was built in 1889 and is an immense hotel with a rather jumbled exterior. This was the heart of the fashionable spa of Harrogate with the Royal Hall, Spa Rooms, Royal Baths and Royal Pump Room all within a short distance. The **Hotel Majestic** dominates Harrogate's skyline, its imposing brick façade and copper dome clearly visible. Built in 1900, it was the last word in opulence and still stands today as one of the country's finest hotels. Inside are palatial rooms, sweeping staircases, marble-clad pillars and beautifully painted murals in the main entrance lounge. The hotel was nearly destroyed by fire in 1924 and was hit by a Nazi bomb in 1940 – thankfully the bomb failed to explode when it landed in one of the bedrooms!

The **Hotel St George** was originally a small cottage that took in visitors to the Old Sulphur Well, becoming the George Inn in the late 18th century when the turnpike between Ripon and Leeds was developed. Gradually enlarged during the 19th century, the various stages of building work can be clearly seen with the oldest Georgian part lying along Ripon Road. The hotel retains many interesting features including a fine 1920s stained glass dome.

The Kursaal, renamed the **Royal Hall** following the Great War, was lavishly built in 1903 to the design of Frank Matcham and Robert Beale to provide entertainment for visitors, once an integral part of the spa experience. Countless famous names have performed here from The Beatles to Elgar and Laurel and Hardy to Vaughan Williams. The frontage and canopy have been recently restored to their original glory, although refurbishment plans are in hand for the interior.

To the south of the Royal Hall once stood Harrogate's finest spa building, the **Royal Spa Concert Rooms**, built in 1835 over the highly prized chalybeate Cheltenham Spring. With six Doric stone columns this classical building proudly stood at the foot of Parliament Street and Ripon Road, with extensive gardens stretching along King's Road. The Spa Rooms were dismantled in 1939 and the area was later redeveloped for the emerging exhibition business. There are plans to build a new permanent exhibition hall on the site which will mirror the former Spa Rooms with six Doric columns, stone facing, glass canopies and an atrium.

The Royal Baths were opened in 1897 by a confident and newly created Municipal Council on the site of the old Montpellier Baths to ensure that Harrogate was at the forefront of spa treatment. The result was the most advanced centre for hydrotherapy in the world offering a score of treatments and baths with numerous varieties of mineral water piped from all over Harrogate. The interior was designed to be lavish with ornate tiling, fittings and decorations; the Turkish Baths were particularly striking. A suite of Peat Baths were added in 1910; however, these were demolished, apart from the ornate waiting room, during the 1930s to make way for the Lounge Hall, Fountain Court and the Western Block in an attempt to revitalise the declining spa. The Royal Baths closed for treatment in 1969; only the Turkish Baths remain open as the last remnant of a proud spa town. At the time of writing the entire Royal Baths are closed whilst plans are drawn up for redevelopment into bars and restaurants.

Opposite the Royal Baths stand the offices of **Harrogate Borough Council** housed in the former New Victoria Baths building of 1871, converted in 1931 for office use. Look up above the entrance and you will see the old motto of the town, *Arx Celebris Fontibus*, which means 'a Citadel famous for its Springs'; today their motto is 'To Be of Service'.

Crescent Gardens provide a pleasant area of greenery in the heart of the town. For almost 200 years this was the site of the Crescent Inn, an early 18th century hostelry originally known by the sign of the Globe and then the Half Moon – it even had its own sulphur spring. Behind the inn stood the original Victoria Baths, the first public baths in the town, built by John Williams in 1832 to an elegant design with Ionic pillars that set the trend for future spa buildings; they were replaced in 1871 by the New Victoria Baths. The Crescent Inn was demolished in the 1890s to make way for the gardens to provide visitors with an area to stroll after visiting the Old Sulphur Well; by the late 19th century this was a very fashionable place to be seen! At the centre of the gardens is the beautiful statue of '**Cupid and Psyche**' within a glazed dome. Made in 1861 by Giovanni Maria Benzoni, this once stood in the gardens of the Spa Rooms before the area was redeveloped during the late 1950s; the statue then 'disappeared' until it was rediscovered in 1989. Note the fine row of buildings with superb stonework along Crescent Road which were once home to the Grosvenor Hotel and have recently been renovated into trendy apartments.

(4) *Head to the right of the Royal Baths along Montpellier Road and follow the road up to reach Montpellier Parade, a traffic roundabout and The Crown Hotel.*

The small octagonal building at the foot of The Ginnel is known as **White Cottage**, possibly the smallest clothes shop in England. This was once the ticket office to the Montpellier Gardens and Baths, part of the Crown Hotel Estate. Several important sulphur springs were discovered here during the 1820s and in 1834 Thackwray, owner of the Crown, built the magnificent Montpellier Baths. These baths were considered for many years to be the very best in the town with suites of tile and marble baths and well-maintained gardens stretching up to Parliament Street. George Dawson bought the Estate in 1869 and subsequently built a new pump room and bandstand and improved the gardens. The Montpellier Baths were swept away in 1897 to make room for the Royal Baths as demand rose for bigger and better treatment facilities. A large part of

the gardens disappeared in the 1930s when the Royal Baths were extended and then again in 1954 to create a car park.

The **Crown Hotel** was once Low Harrogate's premier hotel as its location adjacent to the Old Sulphur Well meant that it quickly became popular with wealthy visitors, although it gained the nickname of 'The Hospital' due to the number of invalids staying there in search of a cure! With its origins in the late 17th century, the hotel prospered under the ownership of the Thackwray family during the late 18th and early 19th centuries. The central portion of the hotel was built in 1847 and the wings added over twenty years later when George Dawson acquired the hotel. Used by the Air Ministry until 1959, the hotel of today has an elegant time-mellowed atmosphere with many features such as superb plasterwork, ornate pillars, open fires and a cast iron staircase.

Montpellier Parade was built in the 1860s as the first venture of George Dawson, Harrogate's influential property developer who also built Prospect and Cambridge Crescents. Sweeping gracefully up Montpellier Hill to reach Parliament Street, Montpellier Parade is home to several high-class shops, including the famous Farrah's Harrogate Toffee. Established in 1840, this toffee is still made to the original recipe, which includes lemon oil to take away the taste of the sulphur water.

(5) *Walk up Cold Bath Road, passing the White Hart Hotel on your right, and continue up the hill until you reach the turning on the left along Queens Road.*

Robin Hood Lane was renamed **Cold Bath Road** in 1880 after St Magnus' Well or the Cold Well, which supposedly soothed eye conditions. It is an ancient route that connected Low Harrogate with Harlow Hill and grew during the coaching era of the late 18th and early 19th century with many inns and lodging houses being built.

The **White Hart Hotel** stands as one of Harrogate's finest buildings constructed in 1847 to a neo-classical design complete with a life-size white hart above the door, although the hotel originated as a coaching inn during the 18th century. The White

Hart Hotel was occupied by the National Health Service after the Second World War and is still owned by the NHS although the University of York now manages it as a hotel, training and conference centre.

The imposing building of the former **Wellington Hotel** is now occupied by several shops, flats and the Honest Lawyer pub. Originally known as the Robin Hood, this hotel was established at the beginning of the 19th century and was extensively rebuilt towards the end of the 19th century. Note the original canopy above the entrance to the pub and the statue of Wellington high up on the building. Several rows of fine Georgian houses line this part of Cold Bath Road, in particular Kensington House, behind which are old courtyards of cottages such as Wellington Square. All that remains of the **Lancaster Hotel**, previously known as Binns' Hotel, where Charles Dickens once stayed, is the northern section of the building complete with a fading advert for the hotel on the gable end. Much of this famous coaching hotel was demolished in the 1960s to make way for a row of nondescript shops. Further along Cold Bath Road stands **The Adelphi**, another old coaching hotel. This hotel became very dilapidated until it was partly demolished in the early 1990s with the finest section of stone façade held up by scaffolding for many years until it was sensitively incorporated into a new development of retirement flats.

(6) *Follow Queens Road then take the first turning on the left along Lancaster Road and follow this to reach West Park Stray, then head right along Beech Grove to reach Otley Road.*

The Stray wraps around the heart of the town providing over 200 acres of open space and fresh air for people to enjoy. In springtime the borders are carpeted with crocus with cherry blossom hanging heavy from the trees, whilst in the evening coloured lights festoon the chestnut trees. This once formed part of the extensive common lands of the Forest of Knaresborough, a Royal hunting forest owned by the Duchy of Lancaster. During the 1760s it was decided to enclose much of the open land of the Forest; however, following the Enclosure Act of 1770 there was great concern over public access to the mineral wells. An Award of 1778 set aside over 200 acres of common land to ensure free access to the mineral springs of High and Low Harrogate, which stated that The Stray should "for ever remain open and unenclosed and all persons whomsoever shall and may have free access at all times to the said springs and be at liberty to use and drink the waters there arising." In 1933 the Council planted flower beds along West Park Stray, contrary to the Enclosure Act. The Stray Defence Association was formed and stood at the local elections, winning seats, and subsequently restored The Stray to its former glory. It has remained open common land ever since, apart from crops and trenches during the Second World War!

(7) Cross over Otley Road and head along Park Avenue opposite. Take the first turning on the left along Park Road and follow this down bearing left to reach The Stray at Trinity Methodist Church. Head across The Stray along the tree-lined path to reach the Prince of Wales roundabout in the shadow of the Prince of Wales Mansions.

With the arrival of the railway in 1848, Harrogate began to grow rapidly as wealthy businessmen were attracted to this fashionable spa town within commuting distance of the West Riding. **West End Park**, also known as The Oval, was developed during the 1870s on land between Leeds Road and Otley Road with spacious houses facing onto a series of wooded gardens and the finest houses fronting onto The Stray. Perhaps some of the building plots were too large as some of the sites remained undeveloped until relatively recently, hence the occasional smaller house. A distinctive landmark is the soaring tower of **Trinity Methodist Church**, built in 1879 opposite which was the site of Harrogate's first station. **Brunswick Station** opened in 1848 as the terminal of a branch line that ran from Church Fenton via Wetherby and the Crimple Valley viaduct. The station was in use until 1862 when a branch line was constructed through the heart of Harrogate to connect the Thirsk and Leeds line at Starbeck with the Church Fenton line and a central station built. **The Prince of Wales Mansions** was first established in 1815 as Hattersley's Hotel on the junction of the Leeds to Ripon turnpike and the ancient route from High Harrogate to Harlow Hill. The hotel flourished with the arrival of the railway and boasted many famous guests including William Wordsworth. The hotel changed names to the Brunswick, then the Prince of Wales, and was greatly extended during the late 19th century; however, this once fine hotel was converted into flats during the 1950s.

(8) *A short detour to England's oldest spa. From the junction of Leeds Road and York Place at the Prince of Wales roundabout follow the path across The Stray lined by mature trees to reach the stone dome of Tewit Well. From here retrace your steps back to the Prince of Wales roundabout.*

Tewit Well is England's oldest spa. In 1571 William Slingsby was riding across the open land of the forest of Knaresborough when he noticed a flock of lapwings, or tewits as they are known locally, drinking from a spring and decided to refresh himself. A well travelled man, he noticed the similarity between this spring water and the waters of Spa in what is now Belgium. He developed the spring and brought it to the attention of Dr Timothy Bright, physician to Elizabeth I – this was the first place in England to be referred to as a 'spa'. The fame of Tewit Well spread rapidly following the publication of Dr Deane's *Spadacrene Anglica* or *The English Spa* in 1626 and it was not long before the medicinal qualities of the waters were exaggerated to almost 'cure all' status. The present stone canopy of 1807 was designed by Thomas Chippindale and originally stood over the Old Sulphur Well in Low Harrogate. Tewit Well was closed in 1971 after 400 years of use and has been neglected ever since; so much so that this historic spring is thought to have been lost.

(9) From the Prince of Wales roundabout head along West Park towards the town centre. As you approach the large War Memorial branch off to the left down Montpellier Hill to reach the Royal Pump Room.

A large stone near to the road along **West Park** marks the boundary of the Leeds to Ripon turnpike constructed during the mid-18th century when several inns and hotels sprang up to cater for the stagecoaches. One of Harrogate's finest Georgian buildings, the **Clarendon Hotel**, once stood to the north of the Prince of Wales Hotel. However, much of this building was demolished in 1972 to make way for a structure that now houses a retail store, although the northern portion remains. The **West Park Hotel** dates from the early 19th century when it was a coaching inn known as the Commercial, and further along West Park is the **Coach and Horses**, a traditional town pub. Until quite recently a traditional pub with a rich history dating back to Victorian times stood here, that was until The Muckles became a mock-Irish pub known as **Scruffy Murphys**.

Just before the junction with Victoria Avenue is a row of four terraced Regency houses, exquisitely built with graceful bay windows and portico entrances. The Victoria Park Company was founded in 1860 by Richard Carter, Richard Ellis and John Richardson who purchased most of the farmland between High and Low Harrogate with the intention of building high-class residential streets for wealthy commuters; **Victoria Avenue** was the showpiece of their project. Today this area represents some of the finest planned urban Victorian development in the world due to the variety and spaciousness of the developments. The incredible **Belvidere House** was the first house to be built on Victoria Avenue in 1861 for a wealthy banker, with the ornate **Congregational Church** across the road finished in 1862. The detached property of **Cathcart House** is famous as the place where the Czarina of Nicholas II stayed when she came to Harrogate to take the waters, keeping in touch with the owners of the house until her untimely death in 1918. The **Harrogate Spa Hotel** occupies a long row of three-storey Georgian houses with fine views across West Park Stray, adjacent to which stands the former **Alexandra Hotel**, an imposing five-storey late Victorian building that now houses the Rat & Parrot pub. A row of Regency houses lead to the **Imperial Hotel**, formerly the Prospect Hotel, which began as a humble lodging house in 1814. Its favourable location overlooking Low Harrogate ensured its success and it was extensively rebuilt in 1859, 1870 and 1936 when additional storeys were added submerging the once-conspicuous central tower.

Montpellier Hill is home to several fine shops and businesses. Of particular note is the old Harrogate Herald Building that now houses the **Slug & Lettuce** café bar, with its old painted advertising signs on the outside of the building announcing 'List of Visitors' once so important to the social life of Harrogate. Montpellier Street leads from the side of the Slug & Lettuce to **Montpellier Mews** at the heart of Harrogate's Antique Quarter with over a score of antique dealers in the vicinity. This complex of stone cottages, with plenty of nooks and crannies, was formerly stabling and accommodation for Harrogate's numerous bath chairs; it is said that at the end of the day the lads would race each other from the top of Montpellier Hill to see who could get here first!

Royal Parade sweeps gracefully from the bottom of Cold Bath Road to the Royal Pump Room, its name derived from the popularity of taking a stroll after drinking the waters. This superb curving row of early Victorian buildings is home to several of Harrogate's finest businesses. Before Royal Parade was developed in the 1840s one of Harrogate's oldest inns, the Bell Tavern, stood on this site. In 1999 The **Old Bell Tavern** opened along Royal Parade on the site of the original 17th century inn; the original cellars still exist which were incorporated into the rebuilding. **David Love Antiques** has a particularly fine original frontage and the **Kay Randle** clothes shop has been in business for at least 40 years catering for the more discerning Harrogate lady.

The Valley Gardens

Start/Finish: Royal Pump Room Museum
Allow 2 hours

(1) *From the Royal Rump Room head over the pedestrian crossing into the Valley Gardens. Follow the highest of the paths to the right that leads through the Sun Colonnade to reach the Sun Pavilion.*

The **Valley Gardens** lie at the end of a swathe of land that cuts into the heart of Low Harrogate from Harlow Hill providing an uninterrupted breath of fresh air and greenery from the countryside into the town centre. The main streamside path through the gardens began life as a humble footpath across fields between the Old Sulphur Well and the Bogs Field with its many mineral springs, once such an important part of the Spa. The land on either side of this path was bought over a period of time,

The Sun Pavilion,
Valley Gardens

mainly towards the end of the 19th century, by the Council who subsequently planted trees, shrubs and flower beds and built bandstands, tearooms and water features along the stream from Harlow Hill for the enjoyment of visitors. Many of these improvements were made for Queen Victoria's Golden Jubilee in 1887 although the fine 18th century houses that once stood adjacent to the main entrance on Well Hill were only pulled down in the 1930s.

The **Sun Colonnade and Sun Pavilion** were opened in 1933 to provide a covered walkway through the Valley Gardens to the Royal Pump Room, a scheme that had been talked about for many years as exercise was considered to be an integral part of the spa treatment and well-heeled visitors needed somewhere sheltered to walk after drinking the waters. The buildings had been neglected for many years prior to closing in 1982 and then they were left to the ravages of the elements until being fully refurbished and reopened in 1998 by the Queen; the Sun Pavilion is noted for its stained glass dome. Dominating the skyline to the right above the Sun Colonnade is Windsor House, previously known as the **Grand Hotel**, one of Harrogate's finest hotels, built in 1903. Many of Harrogate's large hotels were requisitioned during the Second World War; however, the Grand Hotel failed to re-establish itself and has since been transformed into office accommodation.

(2) *After the Sun Pavilion the covered path ends. Continue straight on towards the old Royal Bath Hospital, passing the toilet block, to reach the Old Magnesia Well hidden in trees. Follow the path to the right of the Old Magnesia Well to reach the gates of the old Hospital, where you turn left and follow the stone wall round to the right to join a very clear path near to the tennis courts, marked 'Harlow Carr Gardens 1¼ miles'.*

The imposing buildings of the former **Royal Bath Hospital** dominate this part of the Valley Gardens. The hospital first opened its doors in 1824 with the objective of providing spa treatment for the poor. This was enabled by generous donations from wealthy visitors to the town as well as gifts from George IV

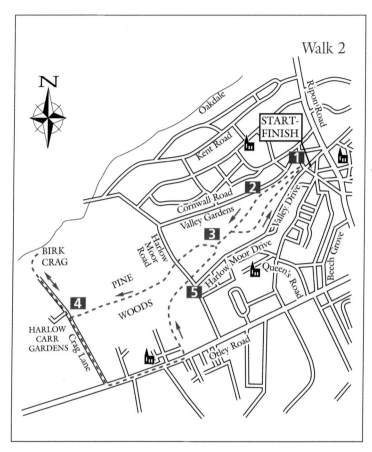

and other members of the aristocracy. Rebuilt in 1889 with a distinct Scottish baronial theme, the Royal Bath Hospital was unceremoniously closed in 1994 since when the old buildings have found a new lease of life as fashionable apartments. Almost hidden by trees is the small gothic pump room of the **Old Magnesia Well**, built in 1858 by the Improvement Commissioners using local sandstone with a steeply pitched slate roof. This building once dispensed the water from the Magnesia Well, which was extremely popular due to its mild nature and effectiveness in curing digestive complaints, or so it was claimed! All around are old well-heads capped by metal covers although two new well-heads have recently been built in the original 18th century design.

(3) *Head along this wide surfaced track gradually heading uphill. At the top of the hill near to a large Crucifix memorial the paths divide; bear to the right along the middle of the three paths (signpost 'Harlow Carr') that passes to the left of the Crucifix heading into the Pine Woods. Follow this path until you reach Harlow Moor Road, cross the road and continue straight on through the woods, skirting a clearing then through more woodland to reach Crag Lane near to the entrance to Harlow Carr Gardens.*

The large crucifix is known as the **Calvary War Memorial**, erected by ex-servicemen following the First World War in memory of their fallen comrades. The **Pine Woods** have cloaked the crown of Harlow Hill since the forest was first formed in 1796 when they were known as King's Plantation. Although dominated by mature pine trees, there is a mixture of deciduous trees and shrubs that combine to offer a glorious display of colour throughout the year. At Crag Lane a short diversion to the right along the road will bring you to the beauty spot of **Birk Crag**. A popular destination since Victorian times, these sandstone crags perched high above Oak Beck offer superb views across Oakdale with the Yorkshire Dales in the distance.

Harlow Carr Gardens are home to the Northern Horticultural Society which opened these gardens in 1950 on land leased from the Council with the main purpose of assessing the suitability of plants for northern conditions. Now covering 68 acres, these nationally important gardens are predominantly used for trial and experimentation purposes and are not planted solely for aesthetic purposes, hence the less formal arrangement of the flower beds. Harlow Carr has vegetable, fruit and flower trails; rock, foliage, winter, scented and heather gardens; alpines, herbaceous, streamside, woodland gardens and five National Collections including rhubarb; there are over 15,000 plants here.

At the heart of the gardens is a small stone building that houses the Study Centre which was originally a bathhouse built in 1844 along with the neighbouring Harrogate Arms (then known as the Harlow Car Hotel) to capitalise on the sulphur springs discovered here in 1734. Hidden in trees above this Study Centre are the six Doric columns and two lions that once graced the front of the Royal Spa Concert Rooms, Harrogate's finest spa building that was demolished in 1939.

(4) *Turn left along Crag Lane to reach the main Otley Road, then head left along this road back into Harrogate over the brow of Harlow Hill. After passing Plantation Road turn left along a track that leads between the Water Tower and Observation Tower. Follow this track through the Harrogate Council Nurseries bearing round to the right to reach Harlow Moor Road again and the Pine Woods.*

One of Harrogate's newest traditional pubs, **The Pine Marten**, is housed in a fine stone house that was originally known as Beckwith Knowle. The surrounding office complex was once home to the CEGB on land sold to them by the owner of Beckwith Knowle, who also sold them his house! Opposite this house stands the small **All Saints Chapel of Ease**, which was built to serve the growing residential area of Harlow Hill in 1870 whose inhabitants were finding the walk to the original St Mary's Church at the bottom of Cold Bath Road rather strenuous! St Mary's was built in 1824, the first church in Low Harrogate; however, the building was declared unsafe in 1904 and a 'new' St Mary's Church was built on Westcliffe Grove in 1916. Note the fine old iron railings and elaborate Victorian gravestones. The rough lane that leads towards the Water Tower on Harlow Hill is known as the **Panoramic Walk** and for good reason as on a clear day the whole of Harrogate can be seen with the Vale of York and the escarpment of the Hambleton Hills as a backdrop with the famous White Horse of Kilburn clearly visible. Opposite the Water Tower stands the tall **Observation Tower** built in the 1820s and now a private residence.

(5) *Cross over Harlow Moor Road and follow the surfaced track ahead*

through the Pine Woods, down Harlow Hill to reach the Bogs Field area of the Valley Gardens near to the Magnesia Pump Room. Continue along the streamside path back to the Royal Pump Room.

The **Bogs Field** is theoretically part of The Stray, protected by the Award of 1778 due to the wealth of springs that rise here. It lies at the heart of the Valley Gardens and is characterised by circular flower beds with a small, central fountain as a feature. It is here that thirty-six of Harrogate's eighty-eight mineral springs rise to the surface. Nowhere else in the world can claim such a diverse range of mineral wells in such close proximity – this small area is globally unique. A fascinating information plaque can be found nearby, complete with a map showing the location of every spring.

Until the Improvement Commissioners improved the wells during the 1850s, many of these springs bubbled up to the surface and ran into the surrounding marshy ground. Metal covers still cap a handful of the springs, although most were sunk beneath the gardens when the spa became redundant in the early 1970s. It was from here that the various mineral waters were piped to the Royal Bath Hospital, Victoria Baths and the Royal Baths for drinking and treatment. To the right is the elegant **Magnesia Pump Room** built in 1895 to replace the Old Magnesia Well. Twice gutted by fire in 1924 and 1983, this now serves as a popular café, beside which is a small boating lake. The streamside path between the Magnesia Pump Room and the Royal Pump Room is known as the **Elgar Walk** named after Edward Elgar who regularly visited Harrogate between 1912 and 1927.

Walk Three

High Harrogate

Start/Finish: Church Square, High Harrogate Stray
Allow 1¹/₂ hours

Mansfield House

(1) *From Church Square, near Christ Church, walk along Park Road passing the church on your left to reach Park Parade, where you turn right all the way to the road junction with Westmoreland Street.*

Church Square is one of Harrogate's most historic sites as this is the only part of The Stray to be built upon, pre-dating the Enclosure Act of 1770. Originally this formed part of a small area of land given to the curate of the adjacent church as a stipend. As it lay at the junction of the ancient routes between Harlow and Bilton, the area was soon built upon. I recommend that you walk around the entire Church Square as there is a wealth of wonderful architecture including **Mansfield House**, Harrogate's first purpose-built theatre dating from 1788 built by the owners of the Granby Hotel to provide entertainment for visitors. The theatre closed in 1830 and is now a private residence. **The Empress** dates back to the 18th century when it was a humble inn known as the Bay Horse although the present building is late Victorian. Georgian, Victorian and modern houses blend perfectly together with a particularly well-designed modern development of apartments.

There has been a church here for over 250 years, perhaps even longer, as this may have been the site of the medieval Chantry Chapel of Bilton-with-Harrogate. Harrogate's first church, dedicated to St John, was built here in 1749 to cater for the spiritual needs of the growing number of visitors to the spa; however, it was often overflowing with worshippers and so the new and larger **Christ Church** was built in 1831. Spend some time exploring as it is a fascinating place – it is also the last resting

Christ Church

ground for many people for whom the 'cure-all' waters had no effect!

Park Parade is one of Harrogate's oldest streets as it once bordered the open common land of the Forest of Knaresborough. It was along here that many of the town's first houses and shops were built. **Number 20** dates from the late 18th century and was the town's first Methodist Chapel, next to which stands **Park House**, a particularly fine building noted for being the home of the last Prince Bishop of Durham. Other houses of note are the **Old Parsonage** and the Georgian **Bilton House**, now the Registry Office. All along Park Parade are superb examples of 18th and 19th century houses built in varying styles but all complementing each other perfectly.

Walker's Passage was once one of the main routes between the old villages of High and Low Harrogate before any connecting roads were built; for many years this was just a footpath across fields. To the right, just off the Jubilee Path across The Stray, stands an oak tree protected by iron railings that was planted in 1902 by **Samson Fox** – an inventor and one of the town's most colourful and philanthropic men – to commemorate the ox roasting on The Stray in celebration of Queen Victoria's Jubilee in 1887 and peace in South Africa in 1902. Park Parade now becomes **Regent Parade**, known as Paradise Row in the early 19th century. This was where many of High Harrogate's first shops were situated until the emphasis shifted to Low and Central Harrogate during the 19th century. Some of these old buildings have been recently restored with contemporary frontages; however, a great deal of work is still required to improve the aesthetic nature of this historic corner of Harrogate. Note the toilet block near to the junction with Westmoreland Street, built above ground in the 1950s contrary to the Stray Act, which states that public conveniences should be built underground if within 75 yards of another building.

(2) *Cross Westmoreland Street and continue along Regent Parade to reach Dragon Parade where you turn right and cross the busy Skipton Road.*

Hidden away down an alley lies **Thompson's Yard**, a rare surviving early-Victorian courtyard development of workshops that was named after a Victorian joiner who once operated here; interestingly there is still a joiner's shop here. Mornington Crescent was where one of Harrogate's most famous hotels once stood. The **Dragon Hotel** developed from a small 17th century inn into a large hotel and gained the nickname of the House of Commons as it was favoured by patrons more interested in the social, rather than the medicinal, aspects of the spa. By the mid-19th century the hotel became redundant as Low Harrogate took the limelight, and the Dragon Estate, which included 53 acres of land, was bought by Joshua Bower in 1855. He planned to develop an area of high-class housing; however, his vision was thwarted by the railway embankment that cut through the estate which meant that the area was not developed until the 1890s. The Stray is at its narrowest here and runs all the way to the Skipton Road railway bridge.

(3) *After crossing Skipton Road, turn right along Dragon View which leads on to Devonshire Place, cross over Claro Road to reach the old Granby Hotel.*

Along with Regent Parade, **Devonshire Place** developed along the fringes of the old common land with many shops and inns opening during the late 18th century. Today this street is in need of restoration as many buildings are in a dilapidated state. The **Devonshire Arms** dates from the 1860s, although it stands on the site of a former small brewery and spirit merchant. The **Black Swan** was rebuilt in 1895 and boasts some fine exterior stonework. **The County** was one of Harrogate's most historic inns with a history that stretched back to at least the 18th century, prospering during the coaching era of the early 19th century when it was known as the Hope Inn. This proud history came to an end in February 2000 when it was converted into a restaurant.

Adjacent to The County stands the magnificent **Dorchester House**, a superbly proportioned three-storey house complete with iron railings that form a first floor gallery. The immense

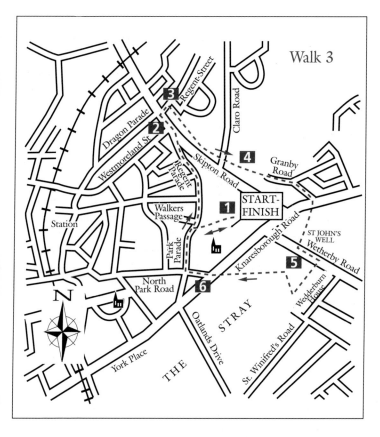

white building of the former **Granby Hotel** is now a residential home known as Granby Court. Dating from the late 17th century, this was once one of the most prestigious addresses in England gaining the nickname of the House of Lords. It was originally known as The Sinking Ship and then The Royal Oak, changing its name to the Granby Hotel in 1795 in honour of the Marquis of Granby who won fame in the Seven Years War. It remained as a hotel until 1995 when, due to disrepair, it became the Granby Court, since when much work has been done to restore and repair the fabric of the building to ensure that it will remain a familiar landmark of High Harrogate for many more years to come.

(4) *Continue along Granby Road to reach the main Knaresborough Road, cross over and head diagonally to the right across The Stray to reach the small pump room of St John's Well.*

St John's Well was discovered in 1631 by Dr Stanhope and was originally called the 'Sweet Spa' due to the pleasant nature of its chalybeate water, later adopting the name of the neighbouring church. This well became more popular than the historic Tewit Well due to its proximity to the amenities of High Harrogate; the site was also less exposed and boggy; at this time The Stray was still rough, open moorland. In 1786 Lord Loughborough paid for a pump room to be erected over the spring to replace the rudimentary stone cover that had been built in 1656. The present building was constructed in 1842 by the Improvement Commissioners to the design of Isaac Shutt, who also designed the Royal Pump Room.

(5) *At St John's Well, turn left along Wetherby Road and then head to the right along Slingsby Walk following the edge of The Stray to reach Wedderburn House. Follow the carriage drive across The Stray from the gates to Wedderburn House and then take the first path that branches off to the left to reach Knaresborough Road near to the toilet block at the junction with North Park Road.*

One of Harrogate's finest and least known houses, **Wedderburn House**, was built in 1786 for Alexander Wedderburn MP, Lord Chancellor of Great Britain from 1793 until 1801 and Lord Loughborough. A regular visitor to the spa of Harrogate, he paid for the first pump room to be built above St John's Well. Designed by the famous architect John Carr, who also designed Harewood House, this beautiful house once stood in extensive grounds along the southern fringes of The Stray complete with its own carriage drive. These lands were sold off for housing development between the wars. The Stray to the front of Wedderburn House was once laid out as a **racecourse**, which can be clearly seen on old maps of 1793. The horse racing was more of a social gathering for the gentlemen who came for the spa season rather than competitive sport. This area is now used by local Sunday morning football teams.

(6) Cross Knaresborough Road and walk along North Park Road directly opposite until you come to Park Parade across your path – the Cedar Court Hotel is a short detour to your left. Turn right here along Park Parade to return to Church Square.

The **Cedar Court Hotel** opened in 1999 after a multi-million pound investment to convert the former Regional Headquarters of the National Health Service back into a hotel, for this is Harrogate's oldest inn – The Queen Hotel. Dating from at least 1687, it was originally built as a coaching inn known as the Queen's Head. It quickly established an enviable reputation, gaining the nickname of the Manchester Warehouse as it became popular with the wealthy mill owners and merchants of the cotton towns and was subsequently enlarged in 1855 and 1861. Inside are many original features, notably some fine ceiling plasterwork. A large block of flats now occupies **Park Place**; the only clue of its former splendour are the mature trees and stone boundary wall for this was once the site of a grand mansion that belonged to William Sheepshanks, a wealthy local landowner. Note the elegant and striking Georgian **White House Hotel**.

Central Harrogate

Start/Finish: Harrogate International Centre, Kings Road
Allow 2 hours

Betty's Tea Rooms

(1) *From the Harrogate International Centre, head down along Kings Road towards the Royal Hall and the Town Centre, then at the traffic junction turn up to the left along Cheltenham Crescent. Follow this road, which soon becomes Cheltenham Parade, to reach the junction with Station Parade at the top of the hill.*

The controversial **Harrogate International Centre**, otherwise known as the Conference Centre, opened in 1982 as a state-of-the-art venue for music, conferences and exhibitions. It is a key player in the economy of Harrogate as a centre for the lucrative conference trade now that the spa is no more than a distant memory. A towering structure of brick, glass and cream-coloured tiles with an adjoining huge hotel cloaked in reflective glass, these buildings will undoubtedly become a much-loved part of the architecture of Harrogate as a stunning example of 1980s' bold design. The neighbouring exhibition halls were developed after 1959 on the site of the former Spa Rooms and associated gardens; note the iron railings along the old boundary wall.

Kings Road assumed its present title in 1910 in honour of King George V. Formerly known as Baker Lane and then Walker Road, this is Harrogate's oldest thoroughfare that originally linked Bilton with Low Harrogate and has been in constant use for at least 600 years. **Cheltenham Parade** was once a tree-lined street of imposing middle-class houses built during the 1870s by renowned Harrogate builder, James Simpson, for the Victoria Park Company to link their developments along Victoria Avenue and Station Parade with Low Harrogate. Today it carries the busy A61 through the heart of Harrogate and is home to several of the town's best restaurants and independent shops. Of particular note is **Pinocchio's Italian Restaurant** as it is housed in an old Music Hall and boasts several superb features including a proscenium arch, gallery and several old adverts for The Empire. Built in 1872 as a Primitive Methodist Chapel, it was converted in 1911 into The Empire Music Hall and then again in 1931 into retail shops. Pinocchio's moved into the building in 1976 and subsequently restored the interior in 1986.

Across the road stands the massive red brick building of **Harrogate Theatre** built in 1900 as the Grand Opera House, as the small tower above the building proudly declares. This plush Victorian theatre is noted for its fine art nouveau frieze in the foyer as well as a wealth of quality plasterwork. This traditional theatre continues to stage a varied programme of productions including their ever-popular Christmas pantomime. The theatre fronts onto the recently pedestrianised **Oxford Street**, once known as Chapel Street, as this was originally a footpath between Low Harrogate and St John's Church at High Harrogate via One Arch, Park View and Walker's Passage. Neighbouring **Beulah Street** is characterised by ornate entrance arches and is home to several interesting shops and buildings, notably the old Salvation Army Citadel on the corner of Beulah Street and Cheltenham Parade, an old Burton's Menswear shop and the grand red brick building, that now houses Intersport, built in 1902 as an arcade. This was one of the first areas in central Harrogate to be built upon as it lay at the junction of paths from York Place and High Harrogate.

(2) *As Cheltenham Parade turns into Station Parade, head straight on across Station Parade to pass through the pedestrian tunnel beneath the railway line known as One Arch. This leads onto Bower Street to reach East Parade, where you turn right all the way to the traffic roundabout at the Odeon Cinema.*

East Parade and Park View once looked across Sheepshanks' Field until the area was infilled with the housing developments of Chelmsford Road and Arthington Avenue between the wars. This area of grass and trees was a planned part of Richard Ellis' development of sturdy Victorian houses that would provide a breath of greenery within the town centre; unfortunately his vision was not shared by later planners. The **Odeon Cinema** is a superb example of art deco architecture and stands as the archetypal 1930s' Odeon building; it was even featured on a 19p stamp in 1996. Built in 1937 to the design of Harry Weedon it is one of the few remaining custom-built cinemas in the country and formed part of Oscar Deutch's vision to 'Entertain Our Nation' (hence the name of the company) by building a cinema in every town. The Harrogate Odeon has a 'twin' at Sutton Coldfield.

(3) *At the roundabout take the second turning on the left along North Park Road and then first right along Marlborough Road to reach Victoria Avenue. Our route now turns right to reach Station Parade; however, a short detour to the left to Queen Parade and back is recommended.*

With the prospect of a more central station to serve Harrogate and the advantages this would bring, the Victoria Park Company was established in 1860 by Richard Carter, Richard Ellis and John Richardson who purchased a vast swathe of land between the old villages of High and Low Harrogate. Their vision was one of spacious, high-class housing for the emerging wealthy classes of the industrial West Riding and **Victoria Avenue** was to be their showpiece. Once a private road with entrance gates and railings, there is still a wealth of incredibly opulent Victorian architecture although one or two of the houses have been replaced over the intervening years by unsympathetic buildings. **Harrogate Baptist Church** was built in 1883 and towers above Victoria Circus, once private gardens with a bandstand for the enjoyment of residents. At the junction with Queen Parade stands the oldest tree in Harrogate, a gnarled oak that was once part of the Forest of Knaresborough. At the junction with Station Parade a short detour to the right brings you to Prince Albert Row, a fine terrace of shops complete with cast iron canopy. This is also the home of **Woods Linen Shop**, a business that has been going strong since 1895 with a history that stretches back to the once flourishing linen industry of Knaresborough during the 18th century.

(4) *Cross Station Parade and continue along Victoria Avenue passing the Library building on your right, after which turn right along Princes Square and follow this across Raglan Street and Albert Street to reach the shopping area of James Street across your path.*

Harrogate Carnegie Library was named after Andrew Carnegie who gave money towards the construction of the library wing of the proposed magnificent neo-Baroque Municipal Palace, which was to have stood on the site of the present Library Gardens. The Library opened in 1906 but this Municipal Palace never materialised, although the keystones still jut out from the gable end of the library building.

Belford Road, opposite the Library, is home to some of Harrogate's most interesting, and least known, buildings. Harrogate's first Infirmary was founded in 1870 along this road and moved into the present **St Peter's School** building in 1883 where it continued until the building became a school in 1937; **Carlingford House** opposite the school was once a nurses' home. George Rogers, a wealthy Bradford textile manufacturer, built the hidden gem of **Roger's Square** in 1868 for the poor of Harrogate and Bradford; the twelve almshouses are still used for their original purpose. A bust of him looks out from beneath the clock tower with the symbol of industry, the beehive, a prominent feature.

On the corner of Princes Square and Victoria Avenue stands **Vanderbilt Court**, a huge mansion that was once the home of George Dawson – builder, developer, Improvement Commissioner, Councillor and one of Harrogate's most important figures. Dawson, along with his architect J. H. Hirst, was responsible for some of the town's finest buildings between 1867 and 1889, including the magnificent Cambridge and Prospect Crescents. **Princes Square** was developed by the Victoria Park Company as a quiet residential square close to the amenities of Central and Low Harrogate and retains a great deal of character with many of the original frontages of these beautiful houses still intact.

(5) *Turn right along James Street to reach Station Parade and the Queen Victoria Memorial. Head left along Station Parade passing the Victoria Shopping Centre after which turn left again along Cambridge Street and follow this down to reach the Cenotaph and St Peter's Church.*

James Street was once regarded as Harrogate's premier shopping

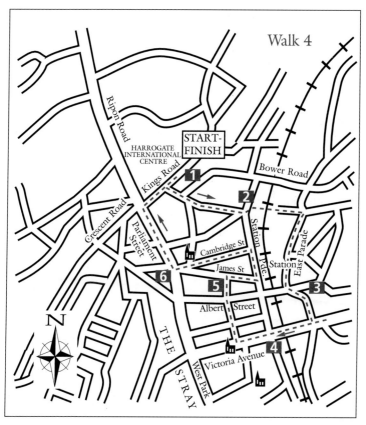

street, a title it may still claim as it is home to many exclusive shops. Of particular note is **Prestons Photographic Shop**, which was founded in 1904 and is probably the oldest family photographic shop in the country; note the collection of very old cameras. **Ogdens Jewellers** is a family business that was founded in 1893 and boasts the finest shop front in the town, unaltered since Edwardian times and an interior to match complete with tables to sit at to discuss your requirements. **Hoopers Department Store** is one of Harrogate's finest, and its predecessor, Marshall and Snelgrove, was a much loved feature of James Street for many years.

The southern section of James Street between Princes Street and Station Parade is made up of an imposing terrace of brick and stone buildings that sweeps up to the finale of the old Station Hotel, a dominating building that still serves as a public house. This row was designed by Hirst in the 1860s for Richard Ellis as an impressive 'first sight' for visitors who had arrived by train, with ornate arches along the ground floor frontages, some of which still remain. **Queen Victoria's Memorial** was built in 1887 in celebration of her Jubilee and was given to the town as a gift by Richard Ellis. The Memorial's gothic canopy was designed by Bown who, along with Hirst and Hiscoe, were the most prominent architects of Victorian Harrogate; the statue of Queen Victoria was created by the respected sculptor Webber. **Copthall Tower** and associated buildings were built in 1965 as a replacement for the fine Victorian station of 1862, which was swept away along with an elegant iron and glass canopy to make way for what was then seen as modern architecture.

The Victoria Shopping Centre opened in 1992 on the site of Harrogate's first Market Hall of 1874. Inspired by Palladio's Basilica at Vicenza and designed by renowned architect David Cullearn, this fine building has significantly improved this part of Harrogate; note the statues depicting 'ordinary' people. **Cambridge Street** developed as the town's main shopping street after the opening of the central train station in 1862, thus moving shops away from High Harrogate.

St Peter's Church has served the spiritual needs of Harrogate since the 1870s when the need for a central church became obvious; the tower was not built until 1926. Inside it is a haven of peace with a beautiful interior noted for its glass and organ.

The Cenotaph, otherwise known as the War Memorial, stands proudly at the centre of what is arguably the most striking area of Harrogate. Ceremoniously unveiled in 1923 as a poignant memorial to the men who lost their lives during the Great War, it stands on land that was once the private gardens of the Prospect, now Imperial, Hotel. It is framed by the great sweeping curves of

George Dawson's **Prospect** and **Cambridge Crescents**, designed by Hirst and reminiscent of a Roman amphitheatre. Prospect Crescent is home to **Allen's** outfitters, a family run business that has been a feature of Harrogate since 1880, although they have only been in this shop since 1891!

(6) *Walk across the gardens of the Cenotaph, across Parliament Street to reach Betty's Tea Rooms, then turn right down Parliament Street to the junction with Kings Road where you head right to return to the Harrogate International Centre.*

Betty's Tea Rooms has been a Harrogate institution since it was first established in 1919 and provides a taste of a bygone era with afternoon tea accompanied by a pianist and views across the gardens of Montpellier. Still a family business, it is noted for its window displays of mouth-watering home-made cakes and pastries as well as a fine array of tea and coffee selected by the family.

The Tea Rooms were originally located on Cambridge Crescent only moving to the former Café Imperial building in the 1970s. If you look above the frontage of the **Edinburgh Woollen Shop** you will notice a beautiful late-18th century stone building with rare bow windows, the oldest in the area.

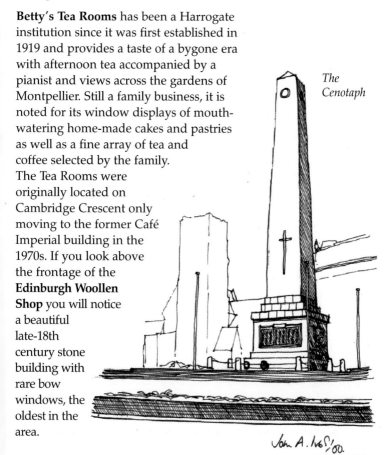

The Cenotaph

John A. Ives '00

Almost unaltered is the old Somerset Hotel that now houses **Yates Wine Lodge**, next to which stands the **Hogshead** public house, aesthetically one of the finest modern buildings in Harrogate, which opened in 1998 on the site of Vani's Restaurant that famously collapsed during renovation work. Across the road are the premises of Harrogate's oldest retail business, that of **A. Fattorini the Jeweller**. Established in 1831, the shop was originally situated in High Harrogate when it only opened for 'The Season', moving to Low Harrogate in 1875 and again to the present site in 1884; it is still a family business.

The Ginnel and Oxford Street once formed part of the footpath between Low Harrogate and the church at High Harrogate, on the corner of which stands a row of fine brick and stone houses built in the 1870s with the old Exchange public house, now Carrington's, virtually intact. **Westminster Arcade**'s ornate frontage and tower still dominates Parliament Street as it has done since 1898. Recently restored it is home to several interesting shops.

Finally, no visit to Harrogate is complete without spending a relaxing hour or two at the **Turkish Baths**, unaltered since the Royal Baths were built in 1897. The original fittings, tiling, baths and steam rooms are all there, still in everyday use, and provide a unique insight into what made the Spa of Harrogate renowned throughout the world.